THE OFFICIAL
TOTTENHAM HOTSPUR™
ANNUAL 2006

A Grange Publication

© 2005. Published by Grange Communications Ltd., Edinburgh, under licence from Tottenham Hotspur Football Club. Printed in the EU.

Photographs © Action Images.

ISBN 1 902704 94 0

TOTTENHAM HOTSPUR™

ROBBIE KEANE

CONTENTS

WELCOME

Welcome to the official Tottenham Hotspur Annual for the 2005/06 season.

We hope you enjoyed your summer holidays and are gearing yourself up for another exciting season at the Lane.

Martin Jol and his players worked wonders last season to push Spurs to the brink of a UEFA Cup place, but just missed out at the final hurdle.

But with Paul Robinson, Ledley King, Michael Carrick and Jermain Defoe at the heart of the side, we have every chance of going one step further this time around.

We hope you enjoy this exciting annual with plenty of information about the players, management and other aspects of the club both on and off the pitch.

Let's hope for another great season under Martin Jol and hope to be celebrating a place in Europe this time next year.

Marc Isaacs
Editor

PLAYER OF THE YEAR
PAUL ROBINSON

PAUL ROBINSON has become England's first-choice goalkeeper since joining Spurs - and what a year he has enjoyed during his opening season at the Lane.

He was always considered as one of the best young keepers in the game during his time at Leeds, but since moving to north London Robinson has improved even further to become a massive hit with the Spurs fans.

In fact, Robinson is so highly adored by supporters that he beat off stiff competition from the likes of Jermain Defoe to earn the crown of Tottenham Player of the Year.

Not a bad achievement by any means, and to add to his wonderful year he is now considered as the best goalkeeper in England.

An impressive 12 clean sheets during the 2004/05 season shows how big his impact was on Spurs as they narrowly missed out on a place in the UEFA Cup.

But Robbo refuses to get carried away by his top displays between the sticks - and sent out a huge thank you to fans for all the support he has received.

Robinson said: *"After the last game of the season the noise coming from the Park Lane end was amazing.*

"It was something special. I had my little girl with me and I almost welled up. You can't find the words to explain the way that you feel when something like that happens.

"The fans have been absolutely brilliant for me this season and I can't thank them enough for their support and the way they've treated me. Hopefully they'll continue to do that and I'll continue to give them the performances.

"When I signed for Spurs, I wanted to prove to the fans that I wanted to be there and want to win things for the club."

Robinson never fails to throw his gloves into the crowd after every home match, giving a lucky fan a special memento of their day at White Hart Lane.

As his bond with the fans continues to grow, everyone at Tottenham hopes he will stay with the club for years to come.

And is Robinson ready for the challenge? Of course he is.

"I have not just come along for the ride," Robbo insists. *"I think the fans can see that. I am a bad loser and they can see the determination and affection I have got for the club already."*

PROFILE

PAUL ROBINSON

Born: Berverley, 15 October 1979

Height: 6'4"

Weight: 14st 7lb

Previous clubs: Leeds United

International caps at end of 2004/05 season: 12

HEAD COACH MARTIN JOL

MARTIN JOL is preparing for his first full-season as Tottenham Head Coach after steering the club to the brink of Europe last season.

Jol arrived at White Hart Lane last season as assistant to Jacques Santini, but took over the reigns when the Frenchman left after just 13 games.

But despite some impressive results in the second-half of the season, Jol will now be aiming to bring silverware back to Spurs and achieve the kind of success he has enjoyed throughout his career.

The Dutchman became well known in England in the 1980s as a tough-tackling midfielder with West Brom and Coventry.

He had begun his career back home in Holland with Den Haag, where he won the Dutch Cup, but also played for German giants Bayern Munich before his spell in England.

At the age of 35, Jol took his first managerial steps back at Den Haag and helped them earn two promotions in three seasons.

He then moved to non-league Scheveningen, but again proved his worth as the club won the championship.

Another trophy came after a switch to Roda as they won the prestigious Dutch Cup - their first piece of silverware in 30 years.

Jol's reputation was further enhanced by a six-year spell at minnows RKC Waalwijk where he turned the team from relegation favourites into European contenders on a shoe-string budget.

Such was his impact at Waalwijk that he was voted Coach of the Year by the Dutch Football Writers in 2001 and took the same award as nominated by his fellow coaches and Dutch players in 2002.

The superb results also brought him to the attention of major clubs across the continent and Manchester United were rumoured to be keen to take him to Old Trafford as assistant manager to Alex Ferguson.

However, Tottenham swooped to secure his services in the summer of 2004 to assist Head Coach Jacques Santini and then took over the role of Head Coach in November 2004.

Jol said: "I've played in England before and it was always my ambition to come back here as a manager. Now I have that chance and I intend making a success of it.

"It is not a minor task, but Spurs are still one of the biggest clubs in Europe. I love it here. We have a good squad and unbelievable spirit."

Spurs legend Chris Hughton, who became Jol's assistant when the Dutchman took over from Santini, added: "He's very, very good to work with, someone who has a real passion for the game.

"I'm sure he was no different in Holland because that's how he is, he enjoys the game.

"I enjoy working with him, He's a passionate man about the game, a big character and that's something that has endeared him to the players, supporters and the press alike."

COACH CHRIS HUGHTON

CHRIS HUGHTON is a familiar face in the White Hart Lane dugout as assistant to Head Coach Martin Jol who led Spurs to ninth place in the Premiership last season.

Hughton has been with the club for most of the past 25 years, first as a player and then as the assistant to various coaches.

Hughton joined the club in 1975 as a player. He featured in the FA Cup final just two years after his debut and was part of the victorious UEFA Cup team in 1984 and picked up 53 caps for the Republic of Ireland.

Following a brief spell away from the club at West Ham, including promotion in 1991, he ended his professional career at Brentford, before returning to White Hart Lane as reserve team boss in 1993.

The Spurs defender served a succession of managers, such as Christian Gross, George Graham and David Pleat, but feels that Martin Jol is the best yet. "Martin has a big personality and he enjoys entertaining football," he said.

His collaboration with Jol since November 2004 got Spurs to the quarter finals of both the Carling and the FA Cup.

Together they nearly pushed the club into the UEFA cup contention with the seventh place still up for grabs on the last day of the season, but missed out at the last hurdle. This year they will be hoping to go one step further.

Hughton's success and results have also earned him the right to be assistant manager of the Irish football team under manager Brian Kerr.

There is a lot to look forward to for Hughton if the national team qualify for next year's World Cup finals in Germany.

Throughout the years the Irishman has proved himself to be a great number two for both club and country.

AUGUST

JERMAIN DEFOE is the main man as Spurs kick off the 2004/05 season under the guidance of new Head Coach Jacques Santini.

An opening day draw with Liverpool gets the show on the road as hotshot Defoe scores a second half equaliser - and Spurs go the rest of the month unbeaten.

Thimothee Atouba, a summer signing from Basle, is soon making an impact on the Tottenham faithful too as he scores the only goal in an away win at Newcastle.

The Cameroon international moved to White Hart Lane alongside some big names including Michael Carrick, Pedro Mendes, Erik Edman, Noe Pamarot and Noureddine Naybet.

The next game sees Spurs travel to West Brom, where Defoe is on target once again in a 1-1 draw.

And the month ends on a high note in front of the Spurs fans as Santini's men prove too strong for Birmingham and battle to a 1-0 win. And you guessed it, that man Defoe hits the net for his third goal of the campaign.

PREMIERSHIP POSITION

4

PREMIERSHIP POSITION

10

SEPTEMBER

PAUL ROBINSON is a key figure between the sticks as Spurs suffer a Premiership goal famine.

Goalless draws at home to Norwich and then Chelsea at Stamford Bridge leave Spurs grateful to their goalkeeper and defenders for proving too tough to break down.

A Carling Cup romp over Oldham soon raises morale however, as Spurs smash six of the best past their League One opponents.

Goran Bunjevcevic, Anthony Gardner, Fredi Kanoute (2) and Robbie Keane all bag their first goals of the season, while Defoe also comes off the bench to get in on the action.

A home clash with Manchester United at the Lane ends in disappointment though, as Spurs fall to a 1-0 defeat which marks their first loss of the season.

OCTOBER

NOE PAMAROT pops up at the perfect time to notch his first ever Spurs goal as he secures a 1-0 win over Everton at Goodison Park.

In a toughly fought clash Pamarot's second half header ends the Toffees' great start to the season and earns Tottenham a welcome three points.

Two weeks later the bubble bursts however, as Portsmouth end any hopes of Santini's side moving up to fourth in the table.

A home defeat to Bolton follows days later, as a Robbie Keane goal is not enough to mark the death of club legend Bill Nicholson with a memorable win.

Revenge is gained over Sam Allardyce's side soon after though, as Spurs win a thrilling Carling Cup tie 4-3 at the Reebok Stadium.

Defoe and Bunjevcevic scored in the opening 90 minutes before the match goes into extra-time. Michael Brown's strike and another from Defoe help edge Spurs through to the fourth round.

The October inconsistency continued unfortunately, and Fulham's 2-0 success resulted in an unwelcome return for Sean Davis - who left Craven Cottage for the Lane months earlier.

PREMIERSHIP POSITION

11

NOVEMBER

JACQUES SANTINI steps down as Head Coach and Martin Jol moves from out of the shadows into the Spurs hotseat.

Jol was thrown straight into the deep end and within 24 hours was on the end of a 3-2 home defeat to Charlton.

A 3-0 Carling Cup win over Burnley comes as a relief thanks to a Defoe strike and Keane brace in the build up to the massive north London derby - which turned out to be one of the games of the season as Spurs were pipped to the line in a nine goal thriller.

Naybet, King, Defoe and Kanoute all got on the scoresheet, but it wasn't enough as Arsenal notched five.

A 1-0 loss at Aston Villa soon followed, but Jol's revival was beginning to take shape and it was not long before he had Tottenham back on track.

Defoe and Kanoute were on target again in a 2-0 win over Middlesbrough to end the month on a high and hand Jol his first Premiership victory since taking over the managerial reins.

13 PREMIERSHIP POSITION

DECEMBER

A vital month in Spurs' season would decide which end of the table they would be battling at - and an unbeaten month put the campaign right back on track.

A Carling Cup penalty shoot-out defeat at the hands of Liverpool does not dishearten Jol's side, and a one goal victory over Blackburn gives the north Londoners something to smile about.

Victory at the City of Manchester Stadium days later thanks to a Kanoute strike secures the first back-to-back win sequence of the season, and inspires the team to a pre-Christmas thrashing over Southampton.

A Defoe hat-trick is just what Spurs fans ordered, while Kanoute and Keane weigh in with strikes during a 5-1 win.

The festive season continues to prove a happy one as Boxing Day success over Norwich follows with a 2-0 win, and a draw with Crystal Palace two days later completes a fantastic unbeaten league record for December.

Defoe already has 14 goals to his name, and Tottenham supporters head into a new year hoping that their season could still be heading somewhere.

PREMIERSHIP POSITION

8

JANUARY

DEAN MARNEY is White Hart Lane's new hero as he scores twice on his full home debut.

Aged just 20, the midfielder opens the scoring as Spurs romp to a 5-2 win over high-flying Everton. And Marney later hits a wonder goal to complete a superb day for the youngster.

Days later Mendes is denied the goal of the season as his effort from the halfway line goes at least a yard over the Manchester United line - but the goal is not given.

The late strike would have been enough to win the game, but Spurs are made to settle for a point.

Keane scores a beauty in the FA Cup as the wonderful run of form continues in a 2-1 win over Brighton in the third round, but successive defeats to eventual champions Chelsea and lowly Crystal Palace follow.

Spurs fail to score in either outing but grab an equaliser in the FA Cup thanks to a Defoe penalty at West Brom to ensure a replay.

PREMIERSHIP POSITION

8

FEBRUARY

MIDO is introduced to Spurs fans after completing a loan deal from Roma - and makes an immediate impact.

Following a disappointing 3-1 defeat at Bolton, striker Mido was the hero against Portsmouth with a double strike during a 3-1 win.

Keane was also on target, and the win helped spur them to more joy in the FA Cup the following week.

Two strikes from Defoe and a Keane penalty were enough to set up a fifth round tie with Nottingham Forest. The Championship side manage to hold Spurs to a 1-1 draw at the Lane and earn a replay at the City Ground.

Fulham were unable to find a way past Robinson in the next big clash as Jol watched his players battle out a 2-0 win.

Reid finally made his debut for his new club, and Spurs continued to hope for a push for a European finish.

PREMIERSHIP POSITION

9

PREMIERSHIP POSITION

8

MARCH

SUPER Irishman Robbie Keane grabs his ninth goal of the season as Spurs march on in the FA Cup. A 3-0 win sees the lads stroll past Forest in a fifth round replay and travel to Newcastle for a mammoth sixth round battle.

Despite a tough battle Spurs come off second best - and lose 1-0 at St James' Park.

In between the Cup schedule Robinson is beaten by a single strike at Southampton to confine the Londoners to a defeat which is hard to take.

And as Charlton win at the Valley by a two goal margin soon after, Jol needed to motivate his players in order to keep any hopes of qualifying for Europe in their sights.

Thankfully that man Defoe was on hand when needed yet again with a vital goal against Man City, before Keane also found the net to secure a much-needed 2-1 victory.

A mixed month had, at least, ended in victory and with two months of the campaign to go there was still everything to play for.

PREMIERSHIP POSITION
7

APRIL

STEPHEN KELLY scores the first goal of his Spurs career and helps his teammates step up their bid for a top seven finish.

The young defender jumps up from the bench and grabs our only goal in a 1-1 draw at Birmingham.

Defoe was the vital scorer eight days later as Tottenham gained revenge over Newcastle for their FA Cup exit just weeks earlier. The super striker capitalised on a mistake by Steve Harper to earn a massive three points.

With morale high Jol's side travel to Liverpool for an epic encounter, in which Michael Dawson makes an impressive debut.

Erik Edman scores a stunning 40 yard goal-of-the-season contender, while Keane also gets in on the action in a 2-2 draw.

A battle with West Brom was never going to be easy with Albion battling for survival, and Mido set up Keane for a second half goal.

Then the big one, and Spurs were bidding to end Arsenals's title hopes at Highbury. A win would have ensured the Gunners could not win the title, but a single goal edged Jol's men out.

MAY

A super individual show from Kanoute helped Spurs keep alive their slim hopes of reaching the UEFA Cup with their 5-1 thrashing of Aston Villa.

The striker scored twice in the first half, while Ledley King also netted before half-time.

Andy Reid grabbed his first goal too, before Kelly rounded off the goal feast. The match also saw Radek Cerny earn his first start in place of the injured Robinson who was to miss the rest of the season with a knee injury.

A clash at Middlesbrough would go a long way to deciding who would secure the final European place, and in a closely fought contest Spurs were pipped at the post.

Tottenham failed to overcome an early George Boateng goal, although Keane came close to earning a point with a superb volley which was saved.

The final day of the season ended in a goalless draw against Blackburn at White Hart Lane, and although Spurs miss out on their dream of playing in Europe the players and fans are upbeat.

Jol has turned around the club's fortunes and led them within sight of the top teams in the country. Now he will be looking to build on a good start and aim high next time around.

2004/05 FACTS AND FIGURES

PREMIERSHIP

First Home Win:
Home Match No. 2 v Birmingham 1-0

First Away Win:
Away Match No. 1 v Newcastle 1-0

First Home Draw:
Home Match No. 1 v Liverpool 1-1

First Away Draw:
Away Match No. 2 v
West Bromwich Albion 1-1

First Home Defeat:
Home Match No. 4 v Manchester
United 0-1

First Away Defeat:
Away Match No. 5 v
Portsmouth 0-1

DOMESTIC CUPS

FA Cup – Progress:
Round 6: Newcastle 0-1

Carling Cup – Progress:
Quarter Finals: Liverpool
(Lost 4-3 on penalties; 1-1)

GOALS

First Premiership Goal:
Jermain Defoe v Liverpool
(Premeiership Match No. 1)

First Premiership Clean Sheet:
Paul Robinson v Newcastle (Away
Match No. 1)

First FA Cup Goal:
Ledley King v Brighton
(Round 3)

First FA Cup Clean Sheet:
Paul Robinson v Nottingham
Forest (Round 5 Replay)

First Carling Cup Goal: Frederic
Kanoute v Oldham (Round 2)

First Carling Cup Clean Sheet:
Kasey Keller v Oldham
(Round 2)

DEBUTS

First New Arrivals:
Robinson, Naybet, Davis,
Mendes, Edman and
Atouba v Liverpool
(Premiership Match
No. 1)

First Academy Player:
Ifil v Liverpool
(Premiership Match
No. 1)

DISCIPLINE

First Yellow Card:
Frederic Kanoute v Liverpool
(Premiership Match No. 1)

First Red Card:
Frederic Kanoute v Bolton
(Away Match No. 14)

THE GOAL
THAT NEVER WAS

ASK any Spurs fan to name their most gutting moment of the season and you can bet Pedro Mendes' name comes up.

You know the date - January 4 2005 - and you know the opponents... Manchester United.

The Spurs were holding their own at Old Trafford and in the dying seconds Mendes spotted United keeper Roy Carroll off his line.

The Portuguese midfielder launched a shot from the right, just outside the centre circle, and it soared past the home defenders who had failed to clear it.

One bounce then Carroll clawed the ball out - but only after the ball had gone almost a foot past the goal line. Cue celebrations! Spurs are set for their first win at Old Trafford since 1989, Mendes is a legend...!

What? The goal wasn't given? But how? Anybody watching could see that the ball had not only crossed the line, it was deep in the goal mouth by the time Carroll got his paws on it! Even Sir Alex Ferguson conceded Spurs were robbed!

Mendes said afterwards he was "sad" the linesman, Rob Lewis, had denied him an Old Trafford goal, adding: "It would have been a superb goal and something to remember, scoring the winner at Old Trafford in that way."

In fairness to the linesman, he was nearer to the halfway line than Mendes and - as he admitted afterwards - he would have had to run faster than Linford Christie to get within sight of the goal line.

In any other season a 0-0 draw at Old Trafford would be seen as a decent result, but in the cold hard light of the end-of- season table, every Spurs fan can see an extra two points would have been a huge help in our quest for European football. Oh well, there is always next season...

23

LEDLEY KING
Q&A

After winning the Peace Cup in Korea during pre-season, how much confidence has that given the squad going into the new Premiership season?

"It was a good experience in South Korea and offered a good chance for the new lads to fit in. The team spirit was great out there and I think that was what won it for us. We are a young group and we really dug deep together - it was great to win it.. Obviously it is pre-season and we won't be getting too excited but I think it was a good confidence booster for us."

The club just missed out on getting into the UEFA Cup this season. How much has it made you extra determined to make sure we qualify for Europe this time round?

"Obviously, it's a massive club and we all want to play at the highest level possible.

"The Premiership has some of the best players in Europe, but the Champions League is the cream of the crop. I would love to play in it.

"People say Rio Ferdinand, Sol Campbell, John Terry are playing Champions League football and that is the highest level of club football there is. I can't argue with that.

"We have promised a lot in previous seasons, but never kicked on but the feeling amongst the lads is really positive that we can go one stage further.

"I am happy at Spurs and want to be part of the future here."

Tottenham more than showed last season they can compete against the very best in the Premiership. How much do the players relish playing against the cream of English football?

"There were a number of big games for us last season that we managed to play very well in. We managed to go on a great run and people said it would be tested against Everton, but we managed to beat them 5-2.

"The same thing happened when we played Manchester United and we should have won that game. We relish playing the big games through the season.

"The supporters were great to us last season, because we have had some tough times. But they stayed with us and it's what we needed."

After making your breakthrough into the England squad, how much would you relish playing in Europe with Tottenham?

"It would be so great for me to play European football and I want to play there as much as the next player.

"The club is big enough and we should be there. It is down to the players to produce the goods and that is all we are striving for."

CROSSWORD

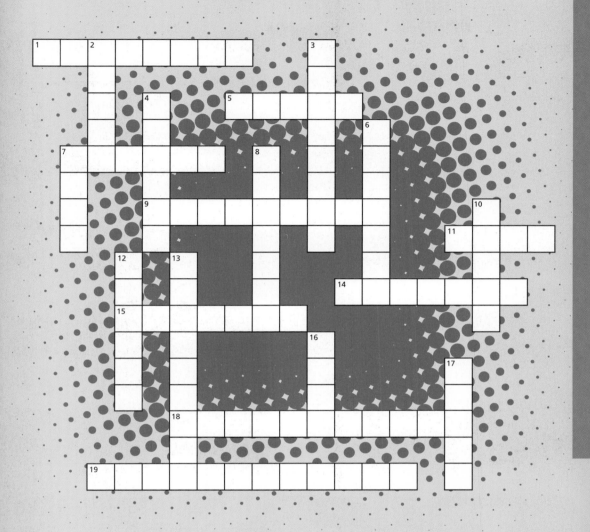

ACROSS

1 Bunjevcevic's birthplace in Yugoslavia? (8)

5 _____ Pleat, in charge of the great Spurs team in 1986-87? (5)

7 Fredi Kanoute was born in this country? (6)

9 Robbie Keane's favourite club as a youngster? (9)

11 Colour of Noe Pamarot's home international shirt? (4)

14 _____ Santini, former Head Coach, in 2004 (7)

15 Jermain Defoe was born here? (7)

18 Reto Ziegler's national country? (11)

19 Danny _____, first international captain to use the defensive wall against Italy in 1957? (12)

DOWN

2 Neil Ruddock's nickname? (5)

3 Keane scored his hundreth goal against _____? (8)

4 French player signs with Spurs in 1997? (6)

6 Spurs lost to this team at the beginning of the year, 2005? (7)

7 Number of goals scored against Everton in January 2005 (4)

8 Vivian _____ helped take the Spurs into the Football league? (7)

10 Clive _____, scored 49 goals in a season in 1987? (5)

12 City where Robbie Keane was born? (6)

13 Bill _____, manager from 1958-74? (9)

16 Pamarot's former French Club? (4)

17 _____ Mendes, joined the Spurs in 2004? (5)

RETO ZIEGLER

LEDLEY KING

TOP SPURS GOALS

1 ERIK EDMAN v LIVERPOOL, (APRIL 16, 2005)

The Swedish defender's spectacular strike was his only goal of the season. After receiving the ball 35-yards out from Liverpool's goal, Edman unleashed a venomous shot which left Reds keeper, Jerzy Dudek, helpless as he watched it sail into the top-right corner.

2 ROBBIE KEANE v BRIGHTON, (JANUARY 08, 2005)

The Ireland international sealed victory for Spurs in this FA Cup tie, when he controlled a long ball from Erik Edman with his back to goal. Keane controlled the ball on his chest, swivelled, and hit a magnificent volley which sailed into the top left corner of the goal.

3 JERMAIN DEFOE v BIRMINGHAM, (AUGUST 28, 2004)

After receiving the ball from Michael Brown, Defoe turned towards goal and began running towards the Birmingham goal. He easily skipped past two defenders leaving them behind and beat Maik Taylor with a beautiful right foot shot from 22 yards that curled inside the keeper's left post.

4 JERMAIN DEFOE v ARSENAL, (NOVEMBER 13, 2004)

With Arsenal leading 3-1, it seemed the north London derby was slipping away from Spurs. But on 61 minutes, Defoe received the ball on the touchline half way inside the Gunners half. The striker weaved himself to the edge of the box and fired an unstoppable shot past Jens Lehmann into the top right of the goal.

5 DEAN MARNEY v EVERTON, (JANUARY 01, 2005)

Everton were losing 4-2 and pushing up the pitch when the youngster received the ball on the half way line. As the Everton defenders backed off, Marney ran towards the goal and from 20-yards, he curled the ball around Yobo and past goalkeeper Richard Wright who was rooted to the spot.

6 THIMOTHEE ATOUBA v NEWCASTLE, (AUGUST 21, 2004)

Spurs were on the break as Jamie Redknapp released Atouba on the left, halfway inside the Newcastle half. The Cameroon international drifted in field and from 25-yards, sent a fantastic curling shot past the diving Shay Given and into the far right side of the goal.

7 THE GOAL THAT NEVER WAS. PEDRO MENDES V MAN UNITED, (JANUARY 04, 2005)

With the match deep into stoppage time, Spurs were denied victory after Pedro Mendes was denied a legitimate goal. He picked the ball up in his own half and tried an audacious lob. Roy Carroll fumbled the shot and only pushed the ball out after it went over the line. The match officials did not see it though and the goal never stood.

AFTER THE LANE

WHERE ARE THEY NOW?

OSSIE ARDILES

Appearances: 311
Goals: 25

Ardiles played for the club between 1978-88. He was signed after starring in the 1978 World Cup.

The arrival of Ardiles coincided with a period of great success for the club.

His midfield combination with Glenn Hoddle brought an FA Cup win.

Ardiles now coaches Tokyo Verdy in Japan's J-League.

JURGEN KLINSMANN

Appearances: 68
Goals: 38

Klinsmann enjoyed two spells at Spurs and was hugely influential in both. He first arrived at the club in 1994, scoring 29 goals in the season.

His second spell in the 1997-98 season saw the team fighting against relegation. He will always remain a Spurs legend.

Now the coach of Germany, Klinsmann will lead his country in the 2006 World Cup finals in his homeland.

GERRY ARMSTRONG

Appearances: 98
Goals: 16

Gerry Armstrong was respected as an honest and hard working player during his time with Spurs. He was not the most glamorous player, but was well known for his very developed sense of humour.

After leaving White Hart Lane, Armstrong spent three successful years in Spain with Real Mallorca, before returning to England with Brighton.

He now works as Assistant Manager with Northern Ireland, and commentates on Sky's coverage of Spanish football.

STEVE PERRYMAN

Appearances: 854
Goals: 39

Steve Perryman is the most loyal player in the history of the club. Between 1969-86 he won two FA Cups, two League cups and 2 UEFA cups.

A tenacious player who provided the grit to complement the likes of Glenn Hoddle around him in some of the best teams Spurs ever produced.

After hanging up his boots, Perryman had spells in coaching with Brentford, and with Ossie Ardiles in Japan. He has since moved upstairs, and is now director of football at Exeter City.

ERIK THORSTVEDT

Appearances: 218

Erik Thorstvedt was seen by fans as the long awaited replacement for Ray Clemence.

After a shaky start, he turned into a real favourite with the fans, and a solid goalkeeper too.

His habit of throwing his gloves into the crowd when he kept a clean sheet summed up his relationship with them. The big Norwegian played in the 1991 FA Cup winning team.

Since retiring as a player, Thorstvedt took up the position of goalkeeping coach with the Norway International Squad and now works in Norwegian television

PAUL STEWART

Appearances: 171
Goals: 37

Paul Stewart played for the club between 1988-92, and will always be remembered for his crucial goal in the 1991 FA Cup final against Nottingham Forest.

His goal got Spurs back into the game after they had lost Paul Gascoigne through injury, had gone behind in the game and missed a penalty in the first half.

Stewart is no longer involved in professional football. He owns his own roofing company, and is currently studying at university for a degree in Spanish.

MICHAEL CARRICK INTERVIEW

MICHAEL CARRICK has got his sights firmly set on helping the club reach the UEFA Cup next season.

Carrick was left heartbroken when the club failed to secure a top seven finish and then missed out on a backdoor route into the competition through the fair play league.

But despite the club's failure to secure European football at White Hart Lane this season, Carrick believes the club have enough quality to take the Premiership by storm.

Carrick said: *"It's been a good season for the club in general. Obviously it was a massive disappointment for us not to get into Europe, but we're moving in the right direction, progressing well and my game has progressed with it.*

"We have got a great squad here and there are a lot of young lads in the team who are just going to improve and get better as time goes on. There are also a few older lads which you need as well.

"But there is a good atmosphere around the place and all the players get on really well with each other.

"There is a great spirit in the camp and I think that shows on the pitch when times are hard how we all stick together and it makes things a lot better.

"There is so much quality in the squad. The future looks very good for us as long as we keep improving. It is great that we have so much competition for places."

Carrick has been handed a new lease of life at White Hart Lane after Martin Jol took over the managerial reins from Jacques Santini.

The former West Ham midfielder struggled to command a regular first-team place during his first few months with the club.

But when Santini resigned from the club, Jol wasted no time in putting the talented midfielder straight into the side and he has been a regular ever since.

And Carrick added: *"Martin Jol has been great for me since he took over and put me into the side."*

"Everyone I have played under has been different in their own way. Martin Jol is certainly a different type of manager – he makes the lads laugh, but is honest with all the players.

"He says things as he sees them and does not hold back which all the players respect him for. Everyone knows where they stand whether it be a good or a bad thing. He has been really good for me.

"Maybe there was a language problem at the start because Jacques Santini could not speak good English and the communication is not the same.

"But Martin Jol speaks better English than most of the lads so it is working out alright for everyone."

Carrick's excellent form for Tottenham last season saw him earn a deserved call-up to the England squad for their trip to the United States during the summer.

And he more than showed Sven Goran Eriksson he can compete at international level with two outstanding performances against the USA and Colombia.

Carrick has now set his targets on playing in the World Cup in Germany in the summer of 2006.

"It's something you work towards getting. This has been a big season for me, a big challenge first of all to get in the Tottenham team on a regular basis and then hopefully doing well enough to get into the England squad.

"Thankfully, it has ended the season quite nicely. Perhaps last time I was with England I didn't appreciate how much it meant. I was handed another chance and it will be great to be involved again.

"Once you have a taste of playing for England it makes you more hungry and you want more of it - especially after the way it was taken away from me.

"I appreciate how special it is now and how much it takes to get in there. When I first earned the call-up, I was only 19 at the time and it was my first full season. Everything was going great for me at the time.

"But since then I have seen the other side of the game and suffered relegation as a player. I know how special it is to be playing back in the Premiership.

"So I do appreciate it even more. Hopefully I am beginning to establish myself in the Tottenham side and things will move on from there."

JERMAIN MAN

1 Did you know that Jermain was born on 7th October 1982 in Beckton, east London?

2 Did you know that Spurs paid West Ham £7m for him in 2004 with Bobby Zamora moving in the opposite direction?

3 Did you know Jermain was on the books of Charlton as a youngster before he signed for West Ham in 1999?

4 Did you know Jermain scored the winning goal on his debut for West Ham in September 2000?

5 Did you know that when he went on loan to Bournemouth he equalled a Football League record by scoring in 11 consecutive games for the club?

6 Did you know he scored on his debut for the England Under-21 side after three seconds when coming on as a substitute against Holland?

7 Did you know that Jermain also scored on his debut for Spurs by scoring after only 13 minutes in the 4-3 win at home to Portsmouth in 2004?

8 Did you know that Jermain was selected for the England squad for their friendly in Sweden in March 2004 and he made his debut as a 12th minute substitute for the injured Darius Vassell?

9 Did you know that Jermain stands at 170 centimeters high and weighs 65 kilograms?

10 Did you know Jermain has won 12 caps for England?

10 FACTS ABOUT JERMAIN DEFOE

SPOT THE BALL (Answers on Page 61)

(a)

(b)

⑫

④

② ① ⑭

⑥ ⑧

①

⑪

⑨

⑤

③

⑦

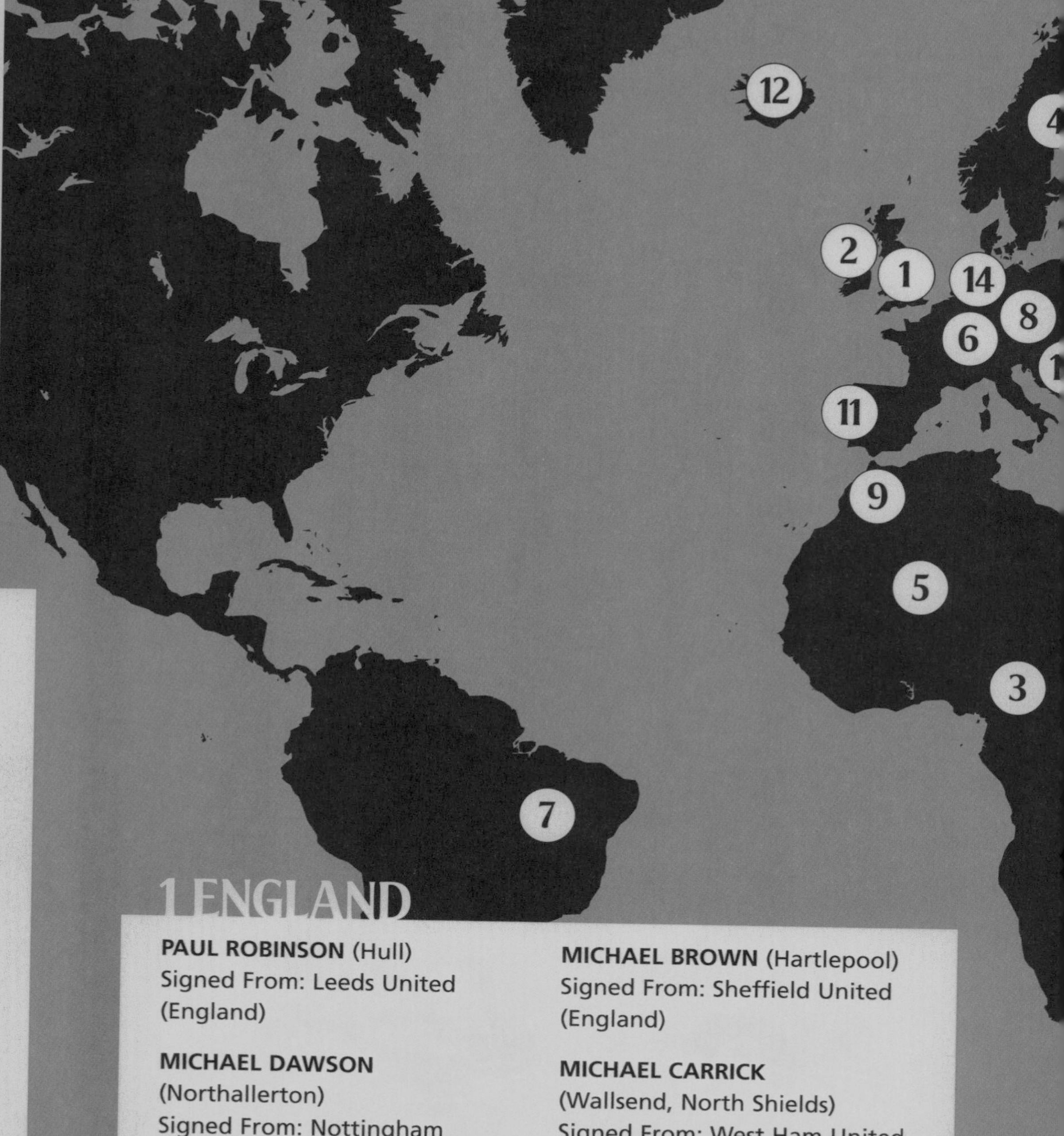

1 ENGLAND

PAUL ROBINSON (Hull)
Signed From: Leeds United
(England)

MICHAEL DAWSON
(Northallerton)
Signed From: Nottingham
Forest (England)

LEDLEY KING (Bow)
Tottenham Hotspur Academy

PHILIP IFIL (London)
Tottenham Hotspur Academy

ANTHONY GARDENER
(Birmingham)
Signed From: Port Vale (England)

SEAN DAVIS (Lambeth)
Signed From: Fulham (England)

MICHAEL BROWN (Hartlepool)
Signed From: Sheffield United
(England)

MICHAEL CARRICK
(Wallsend, North Shields)
Signed From: West Ham United
(England)

DEAN MARNEY (Barking)
Tottenham Hotspur Academy

JERMAIN DEFOE (Beckton)
Signed From: West Ham United
(England)

LEE BARNARD (Romford)
Tottenham Hotspur Academy

34

2 IRELAND

STEPHEN KELLY (Dublin)
Tottenham Hotspur
Academy

ROBBIE KEANE (Dublin)
Signed From: Leeds
United (England)

ANDY REID (Dublin)
Signed From:
Nottingham Forest
(England)

MARK YEATES (Dublin)
Tottenham Hotspur
Academy

3 CAMEROON

NOE PAMAROT
(Fontenay-sous-Bois)
Signed From: Nice (France)

4 SWEDEN

ERIK EDMAN (Huskvarna)
Signed From: Heerenveen
(Holland)

5 MALI

FREDERIK KANOUTE
(Sainte-Foy)
Signed From: West Ham
United (England)

6 SWITZERLAND

RETO ZIEGLER (Gland)
Signed From: Grasshopper
Zurich (Switzerland)

7 BRAZIL

RODRIGO DEFENDI
(Ribeiro Preto)
Signed From: Cruzeiro
(Brazil)

8 CZECH REPUBLIC

RADEK CERNY (Czech Republic)
Signed From: Slavia Prague
(Czech Republic)

9 MOROCCO

NOUREDDINE NAYBET
(Casablanca)
Signed From: Deportivo
La Coruna (Spain)

10 SERBIA & MONTENEGRO

GORAN BUNJEVCEVIC (Karlovac)
Signed From: Red Star Belgrade
(Serbia and Montenegro)

11 PORTUGAL

PEDRO MENDES
(Guimaraes)
Signed From: FC Porto
(Portugal)

12 ICELAND

EMIL HALLFREDSSON (Iceland)
Signed From: FH Hafnarfjordur
(Iceland)

13 EGYPT

HOSSAM AHMED MIDO
(Cairo)
On Loan From:
AS Roma (Italy)

14 HOLLAND

EDGAR DAVIDS (Surinam)
Signed From: Inter Milan (Italy)

A TRIBUTE TO
BILL NICHOLSON

October 23rd 2004 was a sad day for the fans, players and officials of Tottenham Hotspur because it was the day Bill Nicholson passed away.

Younger fans might not know much about Bill Nick, as he was affectionately known throughout the world of football, but suffice to say he is recognized by just about everyone connected with Spurs as the greatest influence in the club's history.

Having joined as a 17-year-old amateur on groundstaff in 1936, Bill went on to become part of the Championship-winning side of 1950-51, playing a total of 341 games for the club and winning just one England cap, when he scored after only 19 seconds against Portugal in 1951.

What followed in his 16-year reign transformed the fortunes of Tottenham, turning them into aristocrats of English football and the first British club to win a European trophy.

Not only did he win trophy after trophy with teams he created over three different periods in the club's history, but he insisted that they play with style, fairness and most importantly made sure they should entertain their most important critics – the fans.

Even now people all over the world consider Bill's Double-winning side of 1960-61 as one of the greatest club teams ever seen. It was the first time of the modern era that a team had won the League and the

FA Cup in the same season, and the fact that Spurs did it in such style and with ease made them so memorable.

His reign as manager certainly got off to a sensational start, with Spurs beating Everton 10-4 in his opening game back in 1958. But it was to be another three seasons before he assembled the team that would make history, as he brought in stars from all over Britain such as Scot Dave Mackay and Welsh winger Cliff Jones. Irish genius Danny Blanchflower was already installed as his inspirational captain.

Having won the Double, Bill then signed Jimmy Greaves, the greatest goalscorer in world football at the time, from AC Milan for £99,999. He famously refused to pay the extra pound that would have made

Greaves English football's first six-figure signing and thus put him under additional pressure.

He need not have worried. 'Gentleman' Jim was an instant hit and went on to become the most prolific scorer in Tottenham's history and one of the greats of English football. He scored as Spurs beat Burnley in the 1962 FA Cup final, but the club narrowly missed out on reaching the European Cup final, losing to Benfica in a controversial semi-final.

But the following year Spurs became the first British side to triumph in Europe, with Greaves scoring twice as they beat Atletico Madrid 5-1 on a memorable night in Rotterdam.

The team soon broke up, with Blanchflower retiring, John White tragically struck dead by lightning and Mackay suffering serious injuries. But the Scot returned to lead Spurs to another FA Cup triumph in 1967, beating Chelsea.

By 1971, Greaves had gone, too, but

Alan Mullery and goalscorer supreme Martin Chivers, started to be successful. They won the League Cup in 1971 and 1973 and the UEFA Cup in 1972, thus becoming the first British side to win two different European trophies.

But it was soon after the UEFA Cup final defeat by Feyenoord in 1974, amid crowd trouble in Rotterdam, that Bill Nick's reign started to come to an end, and he resigned early the following season.

Bill was awarded an OBE in 1975 and was invited back as a consultant in 1976. He was then appointed President in 1991, and continued to live locally and attend games right up until his death after a long illness late last year.

He was held in such esteem that his memorial service at White Hart Lane in November 2004 was attended by almost 10,000 fans as well as the players, managers and officials from six decades of football, all of whom spoke of their love and respect for one of football's true greats.

CHRIS RILEY

Position: Defender
Date of birth: 2.2.88
Place of birth: Enfield
Career: Spurs Academy Scholar
July, 2004.

A Spurs fan who came to the successful community training sessions before being offered a trial. Chris says that he "couldn't imagine playing for another club".

The versatile right-footed defender is confident playing across the back but prefers to be used as a right full-back.

Having already starred for the under-19s, he is a regular England Under-17 international and has made two substitute appearances in the reserves.

ANDREW BARCHAM

Position: Forward
Date of birth: 16.12.86
Place of birth: Basildon
Career: Spurs Academy Scholar
July, 2003.

A former England Under-16 international, Andy is a deadly striker with lightning quick reflexes.

At 5ft 9in he is not the tallest forward, but his pace more than compensates for his lack of height. He loves to run at defenders and has a natural ability to read the game and score from distance.

TOMMY FORECAST

Position: Goalkeeper
Date of birth: 15.10.86
Place of birth: Newham, East London
Career: Spurs Academy Scholar
July, 2003

Tommy has already made his debut for the reserves in a 1-1 draw against Watford.

The 18-year-old produced some excellent saves and comes with a glowing reference from Pat Jennings and Spurs' academy goalkeeping coach, Perry Suckling.

CHARLIE LEE

Position: Midfielder/Defender
Date of birth: 05/01/87
Place of birth: Whitechapel

Solid defender Charlie Lee is already showing huge signs of promise in the Spurs Under-18 side.

The centre-back was part of the squad that reached the semi-finals of the FA Youth Cup last season.

Lee is a composed defender, good in the air and has a reputation as an excellent passer of the ball.

He can also play in midfield and underlined his potential when he scored a brace against Charlton last season.

PHIL IFIL

Position: Defender
Date of birth: 18.11.1986
Place of birth: Park Royal
Career: Spurs Academy Scholar and three first team appearances.

Phil was drafted in as an emergency right-back in the opening fixtures against Liverpool and Newcastle last season where he produced excellent displays.

Great things are expected of the Under-18's captain, who has also represented England at various levels. He is a tough-tackling defender but has a desire to get forward.

CHARLIE DANIELS

Position: Midfield
Date of birth: 7.9.86
Place of birth: Harlow
Career: Norwich City; Spurs Academy Scholar July, 2003.

Having flown the nest at Carrow Road, Charlie is now carving out a reputation as a promising prospect at Spurs.

The left winger is quick and keen to get forward and into the box. He also chips in with some vital goals.

LEIGH MILLS

Position: Defender
Date of birth: 8.2.88
Place of birth: Winchester
Career: Swindon and Spurs Academy Scholar

Leigh showed so much promise while playing for Swindon that Spurs jumped at the chance to sign him.

The centre-back is a commanding presence in defence while also good in the air at set-pieces.

STADIUM FACTS

FOUNDED 1882

GROUND White Hart Lane, Tottenham

STADIUM CAPACITY 36,237

NICKNAME Spurs

STRIP White shirts with navy sleeves, navy shorts, white socks

RECORD ATTENDANCE 75,038, FA Cup, 5 March 1938

LEAGUE WINNERS 1950-51, 1960-61

FA CUP WINNERS 1901, 1921, 1961, 1962, 1967, 1981, 1982, 1991

LEAGUE CUP WINNERS 1971, 1973, 1999

EUROPEAN WINNERS Cup Winners Cup 1962-63, UEFA Cup 1971-72, 1983-84

PREMIERSHIP FINISHES 1992-93 8th, 1993-94 15th, 1994-95 7th, 1995-96 8th, 1996-97 10th, 1997-98 14th, 1998-99 11th, 1999-2000 10th, 2000-01 12th, 2001-02 9th, 2002-03 10th, 2003-04 14th, 2004-05 9th

BIGGEST WIN 9-0 v Bristol Rovers, Division 2, 22.10.1977

BIGGEST DEFEAT 0-7 v Liverpool, Division 1, 2.9.1979

TOP SCORER IN A SEASON Jimmy Greaves, 37, 1962-63

MOST CAREER LEAGUE GOALS Jimmy Greaves, 220, 1961-70

MOST INTERNATIONAL CAPS Pat Jennings, 75 (N. Ireland)

LONGEST UNBEATEN RUN (LEAGUE) 22 matches, (August 1949)

LONGEST TIME WITHOUT A WIN (LEAGUE) 16 matches (December 1934)

RECORD TRANSFER FEE £11,000,000, Sergei Rebrov from Dynamo Kiev

RECORD TRANSFER FEE RECEIVED £5,500,000, Paul Gascoigne to Lazio

STADIUM HISTORY

1882

The Hotspur football club was founded in **1882** by a group of London schoolboys who were inspired by a 15th Century Knight known as Harry Hotspur.

It is thought they formed the club opposite what is now the club shop at the Park Lane end of White Hart Lane. Their first game was a two goal defeat by the Radicals on 30 September **1882**.

In **1883**, and in **1884**, its name was changed to Tottenham Hotspur to avoid confusion with London Hotspur.

The club first tasted competitive football with a 5-2 victory over St Albans in the London Association Cup. Their run in the competition was cut short however, as they crashed to an 8-0 loss at the hands of the Casuals in the next round.

The famous blue and white strip was introduced in **1898**, after experiments with all blue, and various combinations of blue, red, chocolate and gold.

Tottenham Hotspur joined the Football Association in **1889**, but were unable to play in an organised league because they were still an amateur side.

The club's modern home, White Hart Lane, hosted its first match in **1899** as a 30,000 capacity stadium. Notts County were the visitors, and they were soundly beaten 4-1.

Spurs enjoyed their first great victory in the FA Cup of 1901. It was the first of eight triumphs in the competition, and remains the only win by a non-league club.

However, it was not until the **1950-51** season that Spurs first got their hands on the league trophy, and the club's only other title came in **1960-61**.

The club enjoyed European success in the 60s, 70s and 80s, winning the Cup Winners Cup in **1962-63** and the UEFA Cup twice (**1971-72**, **1983-84**).

Since then, another FA Cup win (**1991**), and victory in the **1999** Worthington Cup have been added.

White Hart Lane, Tottenham

YOUNG PLAYER OF THE YEAR

IN a season which saw 20 new players arrive at White Hart Lane, Tottenham managed to un-earth one of the best young talents in the game – **Reto Ziegler**.

The Swiss international arrived in English football last summer from Grasshoppers Zurich and could never have dreamed that he would become a first-team regular so quickly.

Ziegler made his debut as a substitute against Everton last October and went on to make 31 appearances in all competitions.

Head-coach Martin Jol had nothing but praise for the way Ziegler quickly adapted to the rigours of English football and made his way into the full Swiss squad for the World Cup qualifiers against France and Cyprus in March.

And the pacy left-winger hopes he can produce the same form again this season and help Tottenham qualify for a UEFA Cup place.

Ziegler said: "My dream was to play as quickly as possible and as many games as possible and I did that last season.

"It was a dream for me to play. I got into the team, played better and better and now, when I look back, I'm so pleased to have made the decision to come to Spurs.

"The Premier League is very strong and it's not easy for young players over here.

"You have to be ready to play here technically and physically. My qualities were perfect to play here and that's perhaps why I managed to settle so quickly.

"I like this football and it's a pleasure to play in England. Next season my objectives are to have a place in the team, to play as many games as possible again and hopefully play for Europe."

Ziegler has enjoyed a busy summer after playing for Switzerland in the World Youth Championships.

And the talented winger is hopeful that experience will make him an even stronger player when the new 2005/06 season gets underway.

Ziegler added: "I played in front of 80,000 fans against France with lots of Switzerland fans and I will always remember that day.

"I thought I played a good game. Now I'm in the A squad and I hope to stay there and I can only do that by playing well at Tottenham.

"Looking back it was a great season. I had the chance to come here but it's never easy and you need a little luck in your career as well. I'm happy with my season and I just hope I stay clear of injuries."

JUNIOR SECTION

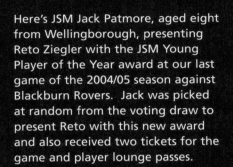

Introducing Chirpy, our club mascot! Many of you may have seen Chirpy leading our Junior Spurs Member (JSM) mascots around White Hart Lane on matchdays and keeping goal at half-time in our 'Shoot for a Holiday' competition, but here's a few things you may not have known about our feathered friend.

Date of birth: Hatched in December 1991.

Nickname: Chirps.

Favourite Colour: Tottenham Blue.

Hobbies: Watching Spurs, socialising with the kids at White Hart Lane

Favourite Holiday resort: Canary Islands/ Turkey

Pro you most respect: Paul Robinson

Favourite sportsperson outside football: Tim Henman

Immediate ambitions: To make all the kids enjoy themselves on matchdays.

Long-term ambitions: To always be remembered as a great Spurs mascot.

Claws cleaned as an apprentice: Cocky Cockerel- our centenary mascot.

Favourite place to be: White Hart Lane/ my nest

Best singer/ band: Sheryl Crow/ The Doves

Favourite karaoke song: Flying without wings by Westlife

Best Spurs song: Cockerel Chorus - *Nice one Cyril*

Favourite car: Nissan Bluebird

Favourite chick: Teri Hatcher

Favourite TV programme: Birds of a Feather

Favourite TV personality: Alan Partridge

Favourite gadget: A Flaptop computer

Advice to a young Cockerel: Follow Spurs to every game.

Best advice received: Avoid fowl play.

Here's JSM Jack Patmore, aged eight from Wellingborough, presenting Reto Ziegler with the JSM Young Player of the Year award at our last game of the 2004/05 season against Blackburn Rovers. Jack was picked at random from the voting draw to present Reto with this new award and also received two tickets for the game and player lounge passes.

But that's just one of the advantages of becoming a JSM!

If you were born after 16 August 1989, here's some more reasons to become a JSM:

Personal club membership card and souvenir pack.

Regular newsletters, including competitions, exclusive player interviews and a message from our JSM president Ledley King.

Priority and discounted home and away tickets subject to availability.

Opportunities to meet the players at exclusive autograph sessions and even lead the team out at White Hart Lane as mascot!

Access to the Spurs Lodge website and email alerts to keep you up to date with all the latest at the club.

Discounts at Spurs Stores as well as on stadium tours, Thomson holidays and Community Coaching courses.

To find out more why not give the Junior Spurs office a call on 0870 420 5000 between 10am and 5pm Monday to Friday, or you can log on to the Spurs website www.spurs.co.uk and click on the 'members' link. Membership fees are £16 (UK), £18 (Europe) and £20 (rest of the world).

SILHOUETTES
GUESS WHO

1

2

(Answers on Page 61)

20.06.2005
TOTTENHAM PLAYER APPEARANCES

1 Paul Robinson
League: 36 starts
FA Cup: 6 starts
League Cup: 2 starts

2 Noureddine Naybet
League: 27 starts, scored 1 goal
FA Cup: 2 starts
League Cup: 2 starts

4 Sean Davis
League: 11 starts, 4 substitute
League Cup: 1 start

5 Goran Bunjevcevic
League: 2 starts, 1 substitute
League Cup: 2 starts,
scored 2 goals

7 Simon Davies
League: 17 starts, 4 substitute
FA Cup: 4 starts, 1 substitute
League Cup: 2 starts,
1 substitute

8 Pedro Mendes
League: 22 starts, 2 subs,
scored 1 goal
FA Cup: 2 starts
League Cup: 2 starts, 2 subs

9 Frederic Kanoute
League: 22 starts, 10 substitute,
scored 7 goals
FA Cup: 5 starts
League Cup: 3 starts,
1 substitute, scored 2 goals

10 Robbie Keane
League: 23 starts, 12 substitute,
scored 11 goals
FA Cup: 3 starts, 3 substitute,
scored 3 goals
League Cup: 3 starts,
1 substitute, scored 3 goals

11 Michael Brown
League: 20 starts, 4 substitute,
scored 1 goal
FA Cup: 6 starts
League Cup: 3 starts,
1 substitute, scored 1 goal

14 Erik Edman
League: 28 starts, scored 1 goal
FA Cup: 2 starts, 1 substitute

15 Mido
League: 4 starts, 5 subs,
scored 2 goals
FA Cup: 2 subs, scored 1 goal

16 Reto Ziegler
League: 12 starts, 11 subs,
scored 1 goal
FA Cup: 5 starts
League Cup: 3 starts

17 Noe Pamarot
League: 23 starts, scored 1 goal
FA Cup: 2 starts, 1 goal
League Cup: 3 starts

18 Jermain Defoe
League: 28 starts, 7 substitutes,
scored 13 goals
FA Cup: 5 starts, scored 4 goals
League Cup: 2 starts,
2 substitutes, scored 5 goals

19 Andy Reid
League: 13 starts, scored 1 goal
FA Cup: 0
League Cup: 0

19 Calum Davenport
League: 1 substitute

20 Michael Dawson
League: 5 starts

23 Michael Carrick
League: 26 starts, 3 substitute
FA cup: 5 starts, 1 substitute
League Cup: 2 starts,
1 substitute

24 Thimothee Atouba
League: 15 starts, 3 substitute,
scored 1 goal
FA Cup: 5 starts
League Cup: 1 start

26 Ledley King
League: 38 starts,
scored 2 goals
FA Cup: 5 starts, scored 1 goal
League Cup: 4 starts

27 Rohan Ricketts
League: 5 starts, 1 sub
League Cup: 1 start, 1 sub

28 Mark Yeates
League: 2 subs
FA Cup: 1 sub

29 Philip Ifil
League: 2 starts
FA Cup: 0
League Cup: 1 substitute

30 Anthony Gardner
League: 8 starts, 9 substitute
FA Cup: 4 starts, 1 substitute
League Cup: 2 starts,
scored 1 goal

31 Dean Marney
League: 3 starts, 2 subs,
scored 2 goals
FA Cup: 3 subs

32 Johnnie Jackson
League: 3 starts, 5 substitute
League Cup: 1 start

34 Stephen Kelly
League: 13 starts, 4 subs,
scored 2 goals
FA Cup: 5 starts
League Cup: 1 start

37 Radek Cerny
League: 2 starts, 1 substitute

Mbulelo Mabizela
League: 1 start
FA Cup: 0
League Cup: 1 start

Kasey Keller
League: 0
FA Cup: 0
League Cup: 2 starts

Jamie Redknapp
League: 9 starts, 5 subs
League Cup: 1 start

Gary Doherty
League: 1 substitute

47

SPURS PROFILES

PAUL ROBINSON GOALKEEPER

Born: 15 October 1979, Beverley England international Robinson joined Spurs from Leeds in May and made his debut against Liverpool in the first game of the 2004-05 season. He has 10 England caps, making his debut in the second half of the 3-1 defeat to Australia in February 2003.

He has become Sven Goran Eriksson's first choice and this season kept clean sheets in World Cup qualifiers against Wales, Azerbaijan and Northern Ireland.

DID YOU KNOW?
Paul is a superstitious person and has a funny ritual before every match: when he is putting his kit on, he always puts the left of everything on first - left sock, left boot and left glove. Of course he makes sure nothing gets LEFT behind!

NOUREDDINE NAYBET DEFENDER

Born: 10 February 1970 Naybet moved to the Lane in August 2004 from Spanish side Deportivo La Coruna - and made his first start for Spurs just 24 hours later!

Never afraid to stick his foot in for a tackle, Naybet has proved a big hit with fans with his never-say-die attitude.

The Moroccan international defender made 31 appearances last season, and hopes to become an even bigger part of Martin Jol's team as they attempt to make it into the UEFA Cup.

SEAN DAVIS MIDFIELDER

Born: 20 September 1979, Lambeth
Spurs welcomed the arrival of former England under 21 captain Davis in the summer of 2004 from Fulham, where he had begun as a trainee. The tough-tackling midfielder is equally at home in attacking and holding roles, but has found his White Hart Lane career blighted by injury. He underwent knee surgery in November 2004 and was expected to be out for the season, but he returned to action after just three months on the sidelines.

DID YOU KNOW?
Before Sean came to Spurs he had played in every Football League Division with Fulham.

GORAN BUNJEVCEVIC
DEFENDER

Born: 17 February 1973, Karlovac, Yugloslavia
Goran earned his reputation as a cultured defender while playing for Red Star Belgrade in his home country of Serbia & Montenegro before he joined Spurs in 2001. He made his debut in a 0-0 draw with Aston Villa and has shown great versatility for Spurs, playing as centre back, left back, left midfield and in centre midfield.

DID YOU KNOW
His nickname is Bunje?

PEDRO MENDES
MIDFIELDER

Born: 26 February 1979, Guimaraes, Portugal
The Champions League winner with Porto - full name Pedro Miguel da Silva Mendes - made White Hart Lane his first home in England and made his debut in the season opener against Liverpool. He scored for the first time in a Spurs shirt in the 5-2 New Years' Day hammering of Everton and three days later his 'goal that never was' against Manchester United became one of the defining moments of Spurs' season.

DID YOU KNOW?
Pedro is a big film buff and takes a portable DVD player on long trips away. Before Porto's big Champion's League final against Monaco in 2004 he and the rest of the team watched 'Troy' to get them in the mood!

FREDERIC KANOUTE STRIKER

Born: 2 September 1977, Sainte-Foy, France
Made a spectacular start to his Spurs career after joining in summer 2003 by scoring seven goals in as many games before he succumbed to injury. He struggled for much of the 2003-04 season but rediscovered his goalscoring touch in the following campaign. He is a Mali international and has represented his country in the African Nations Cup.

DID YOU KNOW?
Fredi's favourite city is Timbuktu! He once travelled there from the Malian capital Bamako and said of the place: *"It was really unusual, and the journey finished with a beautiful desert."*

SPURS PROFILES

ROBBIE KEANE
STRIKER

Born: 8 July 1980, Dublin

Robbie made Spurs his fifth club in August 2002 and ended his first season joint top goal-scorer. He has since wowed fans with almost 50 goals for the club in all competitions. He has been a massive success on the international stage as well, becoming Ireland's all-time top scorer with 25 goals in 61 caps.

DID YOU KNOW?

Robbie is a massive fan of Irish music. He rates Ronan Keating highly but admits to having the odd CD of Irish pub songs in his car.

MICHAEL BROWN MIDFIELDER

Born: 25 January 1977, Hartlepool

Brown signed for Spurs in the January 2004 transfer window from Sheffield United. He began his career at Manchester City and made his Premiership debut against QPR at the beginning of the 1995 season. He is best known to fans for his never say die attitude at the heart of the Tottenham midfield.

DID YOU KNOW?

Michael was sent off in his Premiership debut. He was sent on with 15 minutes to go, but was shown a red card for hauling back a goalbound Andy Impey.

PROFILE

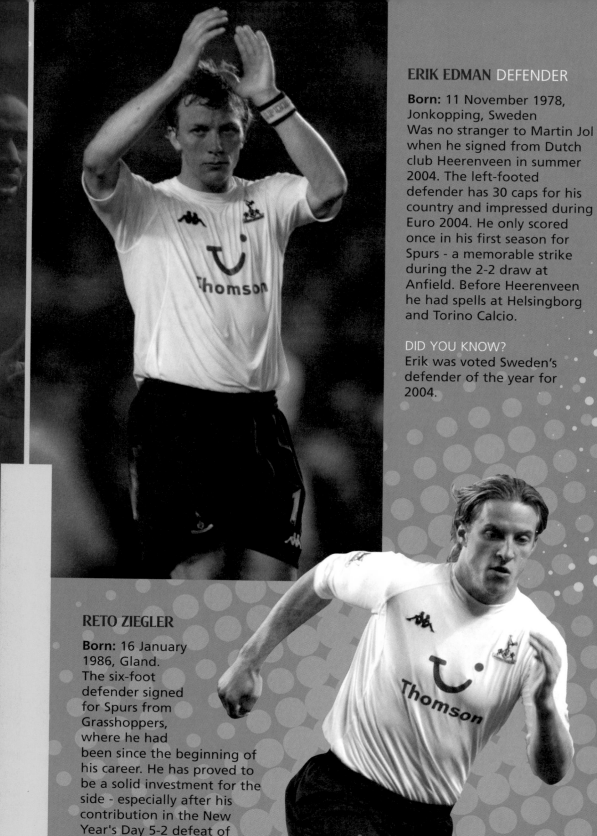

ERIK EDMAN DEFENDER

Born: 11 November 1978, Jonkopping, Sweden
Was no stranger to Martin Jol when he signed from Dutch club Heerenveen in summer 2004. The left-footed defender has 30 caps for his country and impressed during Euro 2004. He only scored once in his first season for Spurs - a memorable strike during the 2-2 draw at Anfield. Before Heerenveen he had spells at Helsingborg and Torino Calcio.

DID YOU KNOW?
Erik was voted Sweden's defender of the year for 2004.

RETO ZIEGLER

Born: 16 January 1986, Gland.
The six-foot defender signed for Spurs from Grasshoppers, where he had been since the beginning of his career. He has proved to be a solid investment for the side - especially after his contribution in the New Year's Day 5-2 defeat of Everton, when he scored his first goal for Spurs.

DID YOU KNOW?
Reto Ziegler played in front of 80,000 fans when Switzerland played France back in March 2005. A day the young winger will always remember during his career.

SPURS PROFILES

NOE PAMAROT DEFENDER

Born: 14 April 1979, Fontenay-sous-Bois, France Spurs gained the Frenchman's services a week into the 2004-05 season, but we were not Noe's first experience of English football - he spent a season on loan at Portsmouth from Nice. The right back began his career at Paris and has been involved in France squads but is yet to make an appearance for his country. Suffered a nasty knee ligament injury which will keep him on the sidelines until Christmas.

DID YOU KNOW?
Noe is a whizz in the kitchen and regularly likes to cook dinner for his wife. He has never tried a jacket potato though!

PROFILE

JERMAIN DEFOE STRIKER

Born: 7 October 1982, Beckton, east London Since signing for Spurs from West Ham minutes before the January 2004 transfer window closed, Jermain has gone from young hopeful to fully-fledged England international. He just missed out on selection for Euro 2004, but you can bet his name will be on Sven Goran Eriksson's squad list for the World Cup - especially after he scored 22 goals for Spurs in his first full season.

DID YOU KNOW?
Jermain is a pretty decent piano player and used to tickle the ivories at school. Now he badgers his sister for tips.

ANDY REID
MIDFIELDER

Born: 29 July 1982, Dublin

After spending seven years at Nottingham Forest, where he began as a trainee, Ireland international Andy joined Spurs on January transfer window deadline day 2005 following speculation which lasted the best part of a year. His versatility in midfield has proven to be an asset and we look forward to some stellar performances from him in the future.

DID YOU KNOW?

Andy has represented his country at four different levels - Under-16, Under-18, Under-21 and senior. He was part of the UEFA U16 Championship-winning Ireland side of 1998.

MICHAEL DAWSON DEFENDER

Born: 18 November 1983, Northallerton

Spurs snapped up the former England Under-21 captain at the end of the 2005 January transfer window - the same time as ex-Forest team mate Andy Reid. Injury kept him from making his debut until April, but he holds promise for seasons to come.

DID YOU KNOW?

Michael may have been a cricketer if his football skills hadn't been up to scratch. He played for North Yorkshire as a schoolboy and built up a good reputation as an all-rounder.

SPURS PROFILES

MICHAEL CARRICK MIDFIELDER

Born: 28 July 1981, Wallsend
Michael signed for Spurs from London neighbours West Ham in the summer of 2004 having graduated from the FA's Lilleshall academy. He won the FA Youth Cup with the Hammers in 1999, but was hit by injury in his final season at Upton Park. He has four England caps and after joining Sven Goran Eriksson's side on their US trip he hopes to regain a regular place in the side before the 2006 World Cup.

DID YOU KNOW?

Michael is afraid of heights! He got the heebie-jeebies on a recent trip to Paris when he went up the Eiffel Tower. According to Michael: "We took the stairs and that was scary. There was just netting between us and a long drop but my missus was laughing at me!"

PROFI

CALUM DAVENPORT

Born: 1 January 1983, Bedford
Calum is an England Under-21 international defender who joined Spurs from Coventry City in August 2004. He was sent on loan to West Ham and Southampton last season to get added first team experience under his belt. The centre-back was handed his Spurs debut in November 2004 when he came on as a substitute against Aston Villa.

DID YOU KNOW?

Calum played his first full game for Spurs' in a reserve fixture against Arsenal?

LEDLEY KING DEFENDER

Born: 12 October 1980, Bow

Ledley has been at Spurs for almost eight years, since he signed as a trainee, and has made over 160 appearances for the club. He has made his mark at international level as well as at White Hart Lane, and is a regular in Sven Goran Eriksson's England squads. His finest hour undoubtedly was at Euro 2004 when he put in a solid perfomance against France.

DID YOU KNOW?
Ledley returned early from Euro 2004, but he had a good excuse - he was in hospital watching his son being born! Coby was born eight weeks prematurely.

STEPHEN KELLY

Born: 06/09/1983
Place of Birth: Dublin

Stephen has become one of most highly-rated full-backs in the Premiership since his debut against Charlton in December 2003. The right-back is captain of the Republic of Ireland Under-21 side and has been included in the full squad. Last season he made 23 league and cup appearances for Spurs and scored his first goal for the club in the 1-1 draw with Birmingham in April 2005.

ANTHONY GARDNER DEFENDER

Born: 10/09/1980
Place of Birth: Stafford
After his early career was hampered by injury, Anthony has came back to become one of the most consistent players at White Hart Lane. His commanding performances at the heart of the Spurs defence saw him win a call-up to the England squad when he made his debut against Sweden in March 2004. The Stafford-born central-defender made his debut for Spurs in March 2001 after signing from Port Vale in January 2000.

DEAN MARNEY

Born: 31/01/1984
Place of Birth: Barking
Having spent a spell on loan with Swindon, Dean has now proved he is worthy of a place in the Tottenham first team. Dean loves to get forward from midfield and even finished second top scorer in the Under-19 side during the 2001/02 season. He broke through to the first team in August 2003 as a substitute against Birmingham before being sent on loan to Queens Park Rangers in January 2004. After another loan move, this time to Gillingham, Marney returned to the Lane on New Year's day scoring twice in the 5-2 win over Everton.

PHIL IFIL DEFENDER

Born: 18/11/1986
Place of Birth: Brent
Phil broke into the Spurs first team last season when he starred against Liverpool and Newcastle, despite being only 17 at the time. He came through the Spurs youth ranks and was captain of the under-18s before earning a call-up to the reserve team where he is now a regular.

DID YOU KNOW?
Phil was a member of England's 2003 World Youth Championships?

SUMMER SIGNINGS

AARON LENNON MIDFIELDER

Born: 16 April 1987

Promising young attacking midfielder - Aaron Lennon signed from Leeds where he made almost 50 league appearances for his home town club, scoring his first goal for the club in the 3-2 win at Sunderland in December 2004. Lennon is just as happy on the wing as he is in central midfield and has a turn of pace that should trouble even the quickest of defenders.

DID YOU KNOW?

Became the youngest ever Premiership player after coming off the bench for Leeds United against Tottenham at White Hart Lane in August 2003 for his senior debut - aged just 16 years and 129 days.

TOM HUDDLESTONE DEFENDER/MIDFIELDER

Born: 28 December 1986, Nottingham

Tom Huddlestone is a versatile young player who played both in midfield and central defence for his old club Derby. Huddlestone broke into the Derby first team aged just 16 and is a regular for the England U-21's and rated as one of the most promising players of his generation.

DID YOU KNOW?

Tom is a big fan of American pool because the pockets are bigger and he plays when he gets an afternoon off.

EDGAR DAVIDS MIDFIELDER

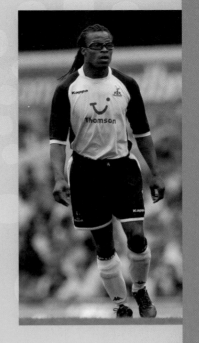

Born: March 13 1973, Paramaribo, Surinam

Started out with Ajax, he went on to win three consecutive league titles, the UEFA Cup and the European Cup with his home town club. A regular for Holland, Davids has had spells at AC Milan, Juventus, Barcelona and Inter Milan before joining Spurs on a free transfer.

DID YOU KNOW?

Davids has appeared in four Champions League Finals.

TEEMU TAINIO ATTACKING MIDFIELDER

Born: 27 November 1979. Tornio, Finland.

At 16 years of age Tainio was spotted in his home town of Tornio and was signed by Valkeakosken Haka. Teemu made his debut in the Finnish League in April 1996. He played the first of his 25 internationals just two years later at Limassol.

DID YOU KNOW?

Tainio spent eight months in the army completing his national service and acted as a postman during his spell.

PAUL STALTERI DEFENDER

Born: 18 October 1977, Etobicoke, Canada,

A Canadian International defender with over 50 national appearances, Stalteri spent eight years with German side Werder Bremen during which time he won the German league and cup double.

DID YOU KNOW?

Stalteri scored on his Bundesliga debut for Bremen against Energie Cottbus in August 2000.

WAYNE ROUTLEDGE MIDFIELDER

Born: 7 January 1985, Sidcup

Wayne joined Spurs from Crystal Palace at the end of last season after turning down a host of other clubs. The right winger is one of the hottest prospects in British football and has been capped for England at Under-16 and Under-19 level.

DID YOU KNOW?

Routledge is a keen PlayStation player and always chooses Edgar Davids when he plays football games.

MARNEY DEBUT

DEAN MARNEY made a dream Premiership impact at the start of 2005 as he struck a sensational double in the thrilling 5-2 win over Everton.

Marney has worked his way through the ranks with Spurs and progressed from the club's Academy before establishing himself in the reserves.

A string of impressive performances left him on the verge of first-team action, and at the start of the year manager Martin Jol gave the youngster his big chance.

Spells on loan at QPR, Gillingham and Swindon - as well as the odd brief outing for Spurs - had given the midfielder a taste of life at the top level.

But this was a chance he was ready to grab with both hands.

Everton were flying high as they travelled to White Hart Lane on New Year's Day, but they were left shocked at the impact made by an unknown 20-year-old.

Marney turned in a sensational display, and took just 16 minutes to make a name for himself. Pedro Mendes linked up well with Robbie Keane, and the Irishman headed forward before Marney sneaked in around the back of the Everton defence to prod the ball beyond Richard Wright's reach.

He celebrated his first Spurs goal with delight and ran into the arms of fans behind the goal. But even better was to come for the White Hart Lane's newest star.

With a piece of brilliant skill he set up Keane for Spurs' fourth goal of the afternoon on 69 minutes, but Marney was saving the perfect moment of brilliance for himself.

With 10 minutes remaining he struck an unstoppable long range drive beyond the grasp of the diving Everton goalkeeper and the ball flew into the net.

Marney had arrived. White Hart Lane had a new hero. And it was a moment the Tottenham faithful would never forget.

Now he has signed a new deal to ensure he will be staying in north London as he attempts to continue his progression in the professional game.

And he is currently on loan at Norwich City, gaining regular first team experience.

QUIZ ANSWERS

CROSSWORD Page 25

```
K A R L O V A C       B
  A         G     D A V I D
  Z         I         R       C
F R A N C E I M     G H T O N   C
I         O   O     O           H
V         L I V E R P O O L     E
E         A   R     O           L A
      D   N   O   N C           B L U E
      U   I   C     E       J A C Q U E S
      B E C K T O N         L     E N
      L   H         N               P
      I   O         I               E
      N   L       S W I T Z E R L A N D
          S                         R
B L A N C H F L O W E R             O
```

SPOT THE BALL Page 33

(a) = 3   (b) = 1

SILHOUETTES Page 46

1 = Robbie Keane   2 = Noe Pamarot

61

ROBBIE KEANE